Outcast From Within

By

Kristie Judah Lee

To my sister, for believing

<u>Preface</u>

There is stillness about the morning that I cannot explain. There is calmness about the ocean drawing to my insides. There is a deceiving quietness about evergreens, making us believe that they are forever young, even as they grow ancient right under our noses. It is the *suchness* of this sense that creates my inner oil. Some people sense it when they are in love. Some sense it through their belief in God. Most of us spend our lives longing for it.

It is a connection, a feeling, rather, a sense that we are all a part of something greater than ourselves. It is a sense that there is a balance to all things, an equilibrium of happiness and heartache that will never lend, to human suffering, too generous a hand. These are the instincts of hope, the naturalness of working to make this world a better place. These poems are my replantings. Cast out from within the scattered islands of unkempt notebooks, these poems are my olive trees to be planted in new soil, in your hands.

Introduction to the 10th Anniversary Edition

I am laying on the beach today, lazily staring into the sand. It is made up of billions of unique pieces, small black stones, smaller tangerine pebbles and even tinier opaque bits. My friend has found an almost microscopic sized seashell and we are pondering what mighty, minut creature could have possibly lived in a shell that small. I smile and happily make up an elementary, playful story about a snail that got too big for its shell and thus decided to leave it behind, braving the great and vast ocean for a bigger home for its behind. We laugh and keep looking at the sand. The further down I look, the more complex the sand becomes. It isn't just sand.

That is what the last ten years have been like for me. Not years, but days and moments and paradigms shifting. Every writer is a little self-indulgent, leaving a bit of themselves on the page for the purposes of catharsis and I am no exception. When I read these pages, I hear soundbites of my life and see the old seashells of my soul. But this is where I have left them.

I have left them here for you to read. I have left them hear for you to love. I have left them here for you to relate to in case you ever find yourself in the places I was ten years ago. I have cast them out from within and as such, I am not in them anymore. You are.

Original Introduction

"There is a difference between self-actualization and self-image actualization. All knowledge is self-knowledge."
       -Bruce Lee

When I was a little girl, I loved to read books. My mother used to take me to the public library and I would spend hours turning thousands upon thousands of pages. I was addicted to the written word, convinced that knowledge was the key to understanding myself. Poetry appeared by way of a sleepy-eyed, blond-haired little boy, too tired from reading Robert Frost to stay awake in front of me during science class. The first metaphor to ever come alive for me came from, " Stopping By Woods on a Snowy Evening". I had no idea words could hide so much in their wings, and I was fascinated by the undertones of violent suicide in such a quiet work. After that it was "The Road Not Taken", several of Maya Angelou's works, Counteen Cullen's collection, Langston Hughes, The Book of Psalms, Nikki Giovanni's love poems, everything written by Sonia Sanchez, Derrick Jensen, and Jelaluddin Rumi of Konya.

    My quest of knowledge has always been a journey towards self, even when I was unaware of it. If I found a character that I admired, I would try to incorporate their qualities into my own life. Indeed, many of my earlier works were copy changes of some of my favorite pieces. Over time, I learned to look inside myself for the qualities of my own character, to write in rhythm with my own self.

    Now my writing is a tool to come closer to others, to build a bridge of understanding from the inside out. I let go of my personal boundaries, in every blank page, to be pushed into a wide, open space of unlimited potential. I was here. I existed fiercely. I lived and loved, suffered and cried, laughed and made sweet music till the very end. Sometimes I found myself lost, and sometimes, when I was lost, I found myself. Not in the mirror, not in the pages, but in the wrinkles of my own hands.

Outcast from Within

My name is J-Bird
I fly solo
in an ocean drowned with my kin
all flapping their wings
incessantly against

THAT WHICH IS ABOVE THEM

some believe she only knows her
sun (son) rises and sets
beside shorelines

They – same ones- pray (prey)
on whales of mat(ter)erealization
with gaping mouths

bending their bit o' sea to their
coral (core all) desires,

under the sea,
a current incurrent reality

scattering static into coherent screams
and no one wonders why it's normal for people
in this country to receive therapy…

Learn how to let go/ be angry/ build
confidence/ maintain/achieve your goals/
keep a journal…

Okay so,
Day 1
Goal 1: flying.

I fly cold
in an ocean kin to my drowning

there is nothing here
She, overwhelming, and I
complete existence

AND NIRVANA IS BEYOND CANDLES

In her nightclub
we are all drunks dancing
to make her wet
the music is flowing from within us
heat vibrating without warmth
there is comfort among our nomadic soul tribe

call it a quest
flying blind
my drowned kin span an ocean

I reply to Autumn's cry
chanting of northward motion

Oh, didn't you get it?

I speak from other hemispheres
rotate 180 and face me
-mirror-

you bite at the heels of dogs
leaving replies unsaid
when she calls

until you have flown both
atmospheres (at most spheres)
you will refuse to appreciate
the woman that tends your wings

WINGSPAN DOES MATTER.

There is no center for saving self

(save for self)

a bed of winds
blind, bold, and blue

she sings a solo to guide through
clouds that daze even a bird's eye view
outcast from within a thousand few.

My name is J-Bird.
Goal 1: flying.

Stained

She dances like dragonflies
drunk with salsa and cilantro

satin shimmering like hidden sunsets
the esoteric glow of green inlets

she begets bloody fabric
from between her legs of confidence

the "click-click" of insteps
clutches the crimson
to the side of her thigh
and it remembers a time
when red was feline

no sick twist of puny purple plums
could wine this vine to bottled decay,

her veins thick, cravings' wick,
sparks nature's flames
-not proclaim-

orientation/motivation with orange obscenities,
peeling skin, sucking citrus,
squeezing sweaty fingerings of flesh
for Saturn's papayas
to go pop

with ripeness
ripping tightness
though blues and greens may taste the rainbow
AND LIKE THIS

her bareback body breathes to breach tips
of territory barricaded by hairlines

behind where her definitive work is written
across an embryo's jaw line

translated from braille to bank side
once every lunar high

she sounds a call to ***war***

no plain flute serenading in ceremony
some simple melody mocking majesty
her dominance is nature's pretense

winds whipping rhythm into tsunami menageries
stretches of snake rattle round fatality
veining the uterus, spooling vitality

sheep's skin cannot cover her insanity

flowing from nipples to bellies, penises to panties
the secret of who we are locked inside her shanty

yet she dances like a dervish and lets her sap fall to the floor,
she dances like a dervish and lets her sap fall to the floor.

Unspoken
for Joe

She laid right there, so calmly
with her matrix
folded
like her long fingers
above her navel.

She had been staring at this long-faced man
since two, quietly listening
to the melody his voice made
with the dying sun outside his bedroom window

naturally there were his
times of silence when he expected
her to say something, anything more
than the conversations strangers finger
when searching for one line
that transcends the gap

somehow they were more than that

a house of sand foundation, made of
chance happenings and intangible threads of
imagination

that perhaps this relationship without logic
could only make passionate sense when

her face gave away nothing except an
avant-garde masterpiece of a reflection
before the light of the siren left to caress
her and the walls' backsides

he knew his performance was not perfect
he had not meant it to be
his words were meant to comfort her

to appoint a certain level of security
to the awkwardness of this situation

in the three weeks they had
known each other

the other world, the sexual world

that which each person leaves
w/ho(l)ly unto themselves until
they feel it necessary to open
the door inside

to speak in the cool tongues of
touch, had yet to be breached

even now, their own
pasts and presents pulled them
in and out of the now's
slowing reaction times way *way* down

a low, less frequent beat

so slow in between
as if something in them
eventually *just had to touch*

instead she sat quietly
occasionally curving her lips
around the open edges of her water glass,
slipping her finger up and down the dew

lost inside the memories of the mistreating men

wondering if another man was really that
which would mend her torn spirit
settling into her character like a summoned sickness

routinely perfecting the art of masks,

even when lying naked together

even when painting the Sistine ceiling on blessed backs
with broad low sweeps of tongue

the words, the words that make the limbed souls
of two people whisper "fuck", "shit" and "oh my God"
 in ancient Aramaic, laughing
like lesbian schoolgirls wrapped around
each others mental orgasms

squeezing at the inner thigh and thought until the hands
run with satisfaction

those were the words missing

or learned not to say, too soon

through trial and error,
error, error, error, and error
Benjamin, Taurean, Jonathan, Brandon,
names synonymous with the way things used to be

why they are no longer

and who is to blame for the haunting that pervades

she thinks

remembers when her father was the only man
who told her about herself

though it could have been just as easy to
mouth the words beautiful, intelligent or gifted

her entire existence was eulogized in worthless, stupid

silence was always her best way to deal
so she fell silent to his assaults

preparing the world of men to greet her
with the same attitude for the next eighteen years
it seems to be wholly apparent now

her first bully was her parents' frown
upon everything she said and did
yet she still reaches out to be
accepted as the perfect kid
by a man who can love her
the way her father never did

and sometimes, belief can be re-built
within a woman broken from birth

and he cannot help but notice
the maybes that cross her forehead
as he uncrosses the folds in her skirt

feeling unnaturally insecure,
as if he were kissing a body of questions

it would be easy to detach himself,
to re-enter his own matrix
through the doors of her thick vulva

losing himself to the force of his past,
rhythmically rotating sixty-nine times inside
but he knows

this is not where their answers lie

and she cannot lie
sex is her human necessity
but her past breaks her future
fractured without her father's intimacy

and he can plainly see
the scars of past fallen stars

ablaze upon her midnight skin,

as his hands uncover the puncture wounds
received by her brother while still in the crib

perhaps, he fancies, God is testing him
though his ideas of God have bounded beyond
believing the chapel bells

there is, yet, an incessant toiling

a low murmuring,
not like the morning call of a new day,
softer, deeper, like the slight
clanging of rusted metal against itself

begging to be breached by
the slave who could come to know
freedom through self-submission

he remembers feeding and clothing
the same mother who spent
his lunch money on an addiction

and even though to this day to try
to breathe her air causes certain constrictions

he *cannot deny,*
love is his human condition

he just doesn't know the words to say
to eliminate this strangeness of himself between women.....

somehow he knows the boundaries blend when
tipsy tongues touch erotic thoughts in seemingly safe h(e)avens,

so he just talks

hoping one day she will not sit

inside his collected life unspoken,
occasionally leaving the opportunity open

so that when she's ready,
she can respond.

On Intimacy
I don't know you
but I can tell you've been hurting.

I know you cry a lot.
I know you cry in your sleep.

I know that every time
you've told someone "I love you"
it has ended badly

I know your domestic is violent.
You've been threatened
beaten
threatened with beatings

I know you're lonely,
you long for friendship

I know that you're afraid to
come close

your walls are mile high
I've watched you painstakingly place
every (*I love you*) brick that
separates you   from   us

I know your memories haunt you.

I don't know you
but I know you
used to laugh a lot more
used to sing a lot more
used to dance a lot more
used to talk a lot more

until the mockery was
just too much,

I know that one day you just shut up

I know that you fight depression.

Struggle for a reason to live

wish life wasn't so complicated

I know you hate yourself,
cut yourself

I know that your self-criticism comes
from a deep place, a dark place
where all the road's lead into one another,
a cyclical miscarriage of self-esteem

I know that you feel lost.
What you are doing just fills
the spaces, the hours, the waiting,

I see you waiting
for death, for love,
prosperity, a place of
peace, your own personal heaven

I know you don't believe in heaven
you've long stopped believing in fairy tales

stopped deserving happiness
started rationalizing your way back to sadness

your misery doesn't like company

two is a crowd
my voice is too loud

I know you don't want to hear what I'm saying
cause you're perfect

you're pretty
you're intelligent
you've got your whole life ahead of you
with the whole world to look forward to

but I know you're listening

you're listening because
you're not very whole

you're listening because you think
I'm going to tell you something
you haven't already heard

something to stop the trembling in your hands,
something to make the coffee, the drugs, the alcohol
-unnecessary-

a resolution to make everything all right,
to make the hurting go away

to make the snow white, to make the sun fall,
to make a crescent ocean, a distilled moon

You know, just as I,
that you are waiting in vain

there is no resolution for you
for any of us

there is only an inner surrendering.
but you know enough
about surrendering

you've surrendered your lifetime
following orders
buckling under societal pressure
trying to "fit in"

I don't know you
but I know that you believe
there is no hope beyond
the olive branch

that your inner oil is all
that feeds you now

I can tell you're wearing thin,
eating less

you think about it daily
giving in

letting go

stopping by the woods on
some snowy evening

you're dramatic like that
longing to be remembered

then you remember
you haven't done anything to merit attention

you're too afraid

What if you did get attention?
Then they'd be happy.
You'd be happy.
You'd be dead, and they?
They'd probably be better off without you.

After all

you're just amusement,
a trivial engagement

no one really takes you seriously

not even you, right?

I don't know you.
No, I don't know you.

No one does.

towards The Inner Bath House

Come, come whoever you are
panderer, priestess, seeker of suchness,
this is not a bridge of false bricks.

There is no need to hide your bruises
before the mountain, though
you stumble again and again

climb, and again, climb.

Following

God is your sculptor.
Why clay, do you fall from form?

Her portfolio does not impress you?

Why does your desire demand form?
Does putty not have purpose as is in God's palms?
Fall into the wrinkles of his flesh,
close your eyes and surrender.

Poem

I have confused myself with
    clarity
and no longer see wisdom.

The base-mean(ing)ts uproot
like old trees in storms
my whole house is without **power**

save for one flashlight
wandering silently through
my thoughts from
living room to sleeping room

looking for a mirror
to bounce back laser constellations

**LET OTHERS KNOW
BODY PRISON CAN BE A HAVEN**

our material life
be our in/ward/in/visible bars

Supplemented diet of dust
Until we starve

From now on,
I EAT LIGHT

and banish my books
into the glint of imperfection.

In Search of Amber

How do you know that horizon
isn't looking out at another horizon?

Gazing as the curved edge of some other world
we're all a part of
just dims away with some
untailored, god-like beauty?

How do you know
the sky doesn't watch
the stars fall over each other?

The sun and moon
sitting and sighing on
some park bench of chance

waiting for the last bit of black hole
to tell them it's time to go inside?

If I go inside that horizon
if I go beyond where I'm boxed in
will I finally find those rocks
kin to my longing?

Or will I,
knowing how sand tends to sky,

find another ocean of

why

how do you know that

why

how do you know that line ain't wide, wide open…

Bending to see

-for Gary

There are simpler ways of saying
"I love you" than what you are doing.
Stop.

Whatever face God wears to you,
does it come and kiss you goodnight
directly on your forehead?

Leaving you dreaming of the redness in her lips?
Or
does she daily come to blow upon your face

the same way she enters
the blades of grass?

The same way she caresses the ocean
or the nothingness of the sky

Do you not have to notice presence to notice her presence?

Let your love for me be part of the movement
that *creates existence*.
Slow. Subtle. Simple.

When you come inside,
do not sigh and say, "Huh, I've had such a long day".
There is no comfort there.

Just
pour the tea.
Make the bed.
Come undercover and leave the without out.

True Healing does not shorten the suchness of pain.
it reminds us of what we have inside to give

think of sex now

pain's path is vulnerability   reminding us

that our life's purpose is no greater
than for the wind to blow through our hair.....

I know you love me.
I can see your pores pouring pools
I can hear your locks whispering to each other

THEY SAY OUR SWEAT MAKES THEM
FONDLE AT THE ROOT WITH LONGING…

unhooked, they mimic our needing to be together
the way our hands grasp,
the Ouija board your thumbs find in my palm

the child you bring out

Can you not see the soft light glowing
behind these eyes?

The amber horizon your smile ripples like a river?

Rising at Dawn
-for Sethye

How is it thou canst rise at dawn?
Hath God herself not disheveled your hair?
Who alive can boast so splendor a spawn
that even fair sunlight no longer seems fair?

For dazzling white doth turn plain blinds a crimson red,
and whereas an abyss would abide with silence in faulty spaces,
sacks of sun strings pluck man's impermanence in tender phrases,
intense, fleeting lyrics, melodious to the sages,

that to deny sensing as a waking hour's devotion,
is like to a lover stopping mid-motion,
how be it that hands glide so gently throughout air,
yet stop and touch not underneath something so fair?

For one who truly loves life cannot stay asleep when God is there,
and to wake too late is to draw evening too near.

The Muted Trumpet

Prayer

Letting the sacred scripture
of her forbidden world
slip from her crimson lips into

the tongues of cavemen
trying translation (trans-change, lay-passively, shun-rejected)
began her end

height faded from existence

a window of water
as if the whole world
could be splashed away

and she began to believe her dimensionless thoughts
and she began to believe…

dreams thickened grips of hands unseen
demanding sing, little bird, sing.

Her One Song (uni-verse)
for Omni

I am aware of rapture.

Its bed lies just beneath
my eyelids, aside my solemnity

I have shunned professions
to profess a truth *shunned*,

the *sense* we hold in common

of the being that is being denied
I am aware

of the elms starving inside
eating the sunlight from which we hide,
I am aware

running from our own feet as guides
so concerned we are with pride
I refuse to accept the montage of
make believe guise

Khrist/**K**omfort/**K**onsumption
sciences of self-preservation

I resonate without you
and so I abandon you

barren be-nots unfertile
who try to save us from
our own September

you force my fruits to ripen
among stolen seasons
soft-bellied and thick-skinned

but I am no saddle cowboy

I cannot be broken in,
only broken…broken…broken…

letting the sacred scripture of
my forbidden world
slip from my crimson lips

as if words could dam pain

from the tongues of cavemen,

though I be blameless,
they turned my name in,
chanting Satan, Satan…

Cry, Freedom, Cry

And I heard the herald morn
sing a temperament tune
that darkened even daylight

there was nothing there
left of her broken body,
pour rain in her viaduct

let the wind whisper blasphemy
for her name's sake

but I saw her eyes
before blowing out candles,
murky in their incandescence

coals burning too hot not to be diamonds

how she, glowed while
sweeping dust from place to place

how, with lips wet,
she wrote of her hidden world,
secret companions and elfish children

she didn't speak her dying words
onto deathbeds

SHE WROTE VOLUMES

but onto flimsy pages,
a dead man' s ears

letting the sacred scripture
of her forbidden world
slip from her crimson lips

as if kisses could somehow
suck ghosts from the tongues of cavemen

as if her wrapped round legs
could elevate them

releasing the voice from within

How trembling thin a line
it must have been

when unknowns prayers of the human mind
cry freedom, cry.

SHE calls me

I.
Serenading
from rooted doorsteps
to orchid awnings

silver lullabies,
a hall of bells
waking the dead
from their bronze coated slumber,
speaking deaf to each other

THEY SAY HER TRUMPETS SUCK TOXIC MILK
FROM SORE COCONUTS AND SAGGING UDDERS

soon her ocean blues will be an
unnoted stream of percussion

-singing-
she liked to peel back her own skin, hey hey
so soggy is her sadness

she liked to rid herself of kin, hey hey
so unnatural is their madness

II.
Resonating
from sex for one
to someone's eyes

reminds our senses,
precious breath, doorways
a cavern of fetishes

waking the dead from

their bronze coated slumber
purring, humming dust to sinew

THEY SAY THE SONG OF SOUL
IS AN EXHALE BETWEEN LOVERS

without flesh, without mind, without
reason, religion, time

-sensing-
a release of raw self, hey hey
so naked is this pleasure

a bending, breaking open, hey hey
so rhythmic without measure.

III.
Calling
from plum budding branches
amidst copper leaves
to father's placenta covered lips

commands caged passions,
a starving child
whimpers in a whorehouse of the selfish

waking the dead from their
bronze coated slumber,
reaching for umbilical cords too soon undone

THEY SAY ALLEYS OF JADED JOHNS AND WET BRICK
ECHO A MESSIAH'S MUTTERS

to hear this song is to saturate our senses with luna(r)cy

speaking-
the dialect of babbling brooks, hey hey
strung from megalith to mountain tower

the cumming of a SHE, HEY HEY
from cunt lips of power.

Worlds of Words

Some things are beyond just words
nigger - cracker - dog - bitch
they're just words

longingly loving lovers lost
just words

whispering winds worrying water
waves
breasts blocking black blood blows
bowel by bowel at a time-
just words
historically

sticks
stones
breaking Jewish bones
sounding moans
in showering graves

clutching cracks in crimson skulls
concentrated crying 962 days

every 3rd slave
weighing in
how   much

skin   it   costs
to   pay back
debts
to western nations
lost
in their own
abundancy

worlds of just words
so fortunate are you,   me

melody
harmony
holding black and white
on the same civil string
keys
the drummer to tap the beat
in this symphony of a reality
needing no lyrics
are oppression-
poverty-
anger-
rebellion-
calamity-
terror-
anarchy-
riot-
streets-
neighborhood-
foreign-
police-
murder-
rape-
black and yellow tape-
injustice- ingested-
news knowing but not speaking
news-
governs-
peaceful-
society-
born-
rebellious-
made-
part-
of systematic (systemic)-
world-
wide

democracy-oppressing poverty-
anger-
rebellion-
calamity-
terror-
anarchy-
riot-
streets-
neighborhood-
foreign-
police-
murder-
rape-
black and yellow tape-
injustice- ingested-
news knowing but not speaking
news-
governs-
peaceful-
society-
born-
rebellious-
made-
part-
of systematic (systemic)-
world-
wide
peasantry

1st 2nd 3rd - minority me
I
Lacking
I-density
In identity
when who what where why
are tossed aside
seen as
just words

symbolic of reality

really who is listening
to be moved not
by what we hear
unshaken by the sound
of the silent scenes

if we stop- listen
it often screams

like an amateur thief
left to die inside his first chimney
"needing second opinion of the
due process given!"

as U.N. civilians
unite nations to speak
leaders wordlessly lead
listening behind
the last in line
picking up what others
rushed past too fast to find

we need leaders
righteous minds
to stop the tape
make us rewind

listen again
to what was being said
between the lines
lies
responsibility
did not pass me
to understand truth is
reality

is something beyond
just words

splattered across the screen
popping off the page
this creative writing
so called "information age"
cuts the floor from our feet in editing
so ignorance will taste right
in the eggs and bacon setting

going about the day
some stop to pray

look up
at sky
ask why

look down
at feet
ask why me

look out
at way
"no purpose today!"
another six-point headline
suffering

in personal cubicle efficiency
shutting the shades
screaming out insecurities-
vulnerabilities
then going back to shoveling
coal
at our station
in the busy bee economy
the "I hate you because you hate me"
ethnic inequalities

the "my way or the highway"
mass religious followings
the movements of peoples
in cycles of conformity

all orchestrated insecurities feeding monopolies

we can't hear or see
ourselves being led
by blind sheep in white clothing
only their lives profiting

but they are moving too fast in front
and cannot assassinate
leaders behind
through the ranks
the wordless will climb
the last
will become first
in due time

listen

it's already
happening

worlds of words are collapsing
as stars
rearranging reveals
twinkles in enlightened
eyes

leaders listen to the skies
for things beyond
just words.

*This poem can be read vertically or horizontally for the first two pages. Enjoy.

Bombs over Baghdad

Let us end it here
freeze frame the bullets
in front of my chest
and set to rest
your ways of violence

in hiding we find our voice
in the vulgar language
of our hands

the cuneiform has changed
but the marks remain the same
from bruising bodies
to bombing Baghdad

the pen is you

inked with oil from foreign lands
you stain your hands

with drips of us

poetic prose in high demand
laced with lies
embalmed in applause

a whole race ringing
with your ignorant songs

but the dead have their own language

the percussive roar of stillborns
(breathe…)
babble Babylon into nothingness
building bridges to a world

without your hues

a mountain of hieroglyphs carved in ice

for brother, though you once
lived amongst us

our tongue, not yours,
created these centuries

you have bent the light
from the shadow of our hands

long enough

the coming sun will bury you
in your rotted rhetoric

and it is then you will know
that this is only the beginning.

Poem

We met on the train
talkin' bout weather
whatever

anyway
we ended up
making great conversation
that lasted…

till now

when there is no more to say

About the Author

Kristie Judah Lee is an award winning poet, scientist and spiritual community leader. At the age of sixteen, she was a member of the National Championship Detroit Poetry Slam team. She went on to publish her first collection of poetry, Outcast From Within, at the age of twenty. She has lectured at schools and universities all over the world, including France, Zambia, and South Africa, promoting mathematical, scientific and creative literacy to children, adults and teachers alike. She obtained her Bachelor's Degree from Hampton University in 2006, majoring in Physics, minoring in Mathematics and Earth, Space and Atmospheric Sciences. She is also a published scientist and has lectured before the National Oceanic and Atmospheric Association, the IEEE Geoscience and Remote Sensing Society and the Center for European Nuclear Research. Currently, she teaches mathematics in the Detroit and is pursuing her teaching certificate to teach English as a second language in India. A prayer chaplain since 2009, her writing focuses on the nature of higher consciousness and the connection of physical and spiritual realms. Her new collection of poetry, *Rage Bursts Into Beautiful*, is scheduled to be released in the beginning of 2016. She enjoys yoga, meditation and learning to play the guitar.

www.ingramcontent.com/pod-product-compliance
Lightning Source LLC
Chambersburg PA
CBHW031218090426
42736CB00009B/972